What Do You Mean?

Communication Isn't Easy

Library of Congress Cataloging-in-Publication Data

Atkinson, Mary, 1966-
   What do you mean? : communication isn't easy / by Mary Atkinson.
      p. cm.
   Includes index.
   ISBN-10: 0-531-17571-5 (lib. bdg.)
   ISBN-13: 978-0-531-17571-2 (lib. bdg.)
   ISBN-10: 0-531-18811-6 (pbk.)
   ISBN-13: 978-0-531-18811-8 (pbk.)
   1. English language--History--Juvenile literature. I. Title.

   PE1075.A76 2007
   420'.9--dc22

2007019984

Published in 2008 by Children's Press, an imprint of Scholastic Inc.,
557 Broadway, New York, New York 10012
www.scholastic.com

08 09 10 11 12 13 14 15 16 17
10 9 8 7 6 5 4 3 2 1

Printed in China through Colorcraft Ltd., Hong Kong

Author: Mary Atkinson
Educational Consultant: Ian Morrison
Editor: Mary Atkinson
Designer: Amy Lam
Illustrator: Janine Dawson
Photo Researcher: Jamshed Mistry

Photographs by: akg-images (Viking ship, pp. 10–11); **Big Stock Photo** (cover; boys and Hispanic
girl, p. 7; p. 19; pp. 21–22; girl with cell phone, p. 31); **Getty Images** (p. 3; Jane Austen, p. 13;
Princess Haya, medieval princess, p. 16; p. 24; boy with binoculars, p. 29; medieval baker, p. 29);
Ingram Image Library (p. 27; bee, p. 29); **Jennifer and Brian Lupton** (teenagers, pp. 32–33);
Oxford University Press (cover of *Jane Austen – Selected Letters* edited by Vivien Jones (2004),
p. 30. By permission of Oxford University Press. Cover art © Photolibrary/Mary Evans); **Penguin
Group UK:** front cover of *The Letters of Vincent van Gogh* selected by Ronald de Leeuw, translated
by Arnold Pomerans (Penguin, 1996) Translation © Arnold Pomerans, 1996. Reproduced by
permission of Penguin Books Ltd., p. 30); **Photodisc** (girl, p. 29); **Photolibrary** (Shakespeare play,
p. 13; Inuit children, p. 25); **RubberBall** (African-American girl, p. 8); **Stock.Xchng** (p. 5, p. 34);
Tranz/Corbis (William I, p. 11; p. 12; p. 15; blond girl, p. 16; p. 28; girls with cell phone,
pp. 32–33)

All illustrations and other photographs © Weldon Owen Education Inc.

What Do You Mean?

Communication Isn't Easy

Mary Atkinson

THE CAT'S PAJAMAS

I WANT TO PICK YOUR BRAIN

BRING A DISH

THE RAT RACE

FOLLOW YOUR NOSE

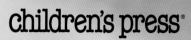

children's press®

An imprint of Scholastic Inc.

NEW YORK • TORONTO • LONDON • AUCKLAND • SYDNEY
MEXICO CITY • NEW DELHI • HONG KONG
DANBURY, CONNECTICUT

CHECK THESE OUT!

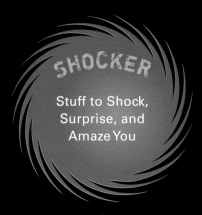

SHOCKER

Stuff to Shock,
Surprise, and
Amaze You

Quick Recaps
and Notable
Notes

Word Stunners
and Other Oddities

The Heads-Up
on Expert Reading

Links to More
Information

CONTENTS

grammar the rules of a language that say how words can be combined to make sentences

linguist (*LING gwist*) a person who studies the way languages work

literally word for word; meaning exactly what the words themselves mean

pronounce to say a word in a particular way

punctuation (*pungk choo AY shun*) written marks, such as periods and commas, that help make writing easier to understand

slang informal language, often the lingo of a specific group of people that has not yet been accepted by most people as part of the language

synonym (*SIN uh nim*) a word whose meaning is the same or nearly the same as that of another word. *Sofa* and *couch* are synonyms.

· ·

For additional vocabulary, see Glossary on page 34.

The opposite of *literal* is *figurative*. An example of figurative language is: *He threw himself on the mercy of the court*. He didn't literally do this, he just wanted the judge to go easy!

English is a language you can have fun with. It has more words than any other language. There are many ways you can put a thought into words in English. If you are meeting friends, for example, there are many different ways you could greet them. The word you pick depends on who you are, your mood, and where you live. However, English is also a tricky language. Consider the word *one*. Would you guess that it is spelled *o-n-e* if you simply heard the word? Now think about this sentence: *I want to pick your brain.* It could be very scary indeed if you didn't know that it really means, "I want to hear what you think about something."

We can never learn all there is to know about the English language. It is constantly changing. New words, such as *webmaster* and *blog*, are invented. Old words, such as *spiffy* and *spurrier,* are hardly ever used. If you move to a different English-speaking place, you often need to learn new words. For example, a *sidewalk* can also be called a *pavement* or a *footpath* depending on where you live. Why is English so varied and so strange? To find out, you need to know a little about its history.

The English-Speaking World

Canada

British Isles

U.S.A.

ASIA

AFRICA

SOUTH AMERICA

India

Australia

South Africa

New Zealand

Countries in which English is the official language or one of the main languages

Countries in which English is spoken widely but is not one of the main languages

In Days of Yore

The history of the English language is a history of battles and invasions. Invaders from Germany and the Netherlands settled in England about 1,600 years ago. These people spoke some very old forms of German. In time, their languages merged into a language that we call Anglo-Saxon, or Old English.

Over the next 500 years, other people came to England and brought their languages with them. Religious **monks** brought **Latin**. **Viking** invaders brought a language called Old Norse. Then, in 1066, the **Normans** conquered England. Their language, Anglo-Norman, became the language of the country's rulers. Over time, all these languages mixed with Old English. They all changed it, helping to make English what it is today.

The word *Yore* in the heading was new to me. After reading the page, I guessed that it means something like "olden days." Many unfamiliar words can be figured out without using a dictionary.

400s A.D.	597 A.D.	800s and 900s A.D.
Invaders from Germany and the Netherlands settle in England. Their languages merge into Anglo-Saxon, or Old English.	St. Augustine and other monks come to England from Rome. They bring Christianity and the Latin language with them.	Vikings from Scandinavia invade England. Some of their Old Norse words, such as *score*, *sick*, and *take*, enter the language.

The Viking raids led to many fierce battles. However, there were also times of peace when the Vikings and Anglo-Saxons traded with one another and learned some of each other's languages.

William I (1028–1087) was the first Anglo-Norman king of England.

1066–1400s

Invaders from France take over England. They speak a form of old French called Anglo-Norman. It eventually mixes with Old English to create Middle English.

Today, we use many Anglo-Saxon and Anglo-Norman **synonyms**. Do you think the Anglo-Saxon or the Anglo-Norman words seem fancier?

Anglo-Saxon	Anglo-Norman
ask	inquire
driver	chauffeur
come	arrive
small	petite
house	mansion
trip	tour
begin	commence
hide	conceal

Old, Middle, and Modern

The English spoken by the first English-speakers was very different from today's English. You probably wouldn't even recognize it as English. For example, take *Hwæt sceal ic singan?* It means, *What shall I sing?* These words come from a book written in the late 800s A.D.

Slowly, and bit by bit, English changed. **Linguists** recognize three main stages in the development of the language: Old English, Middle English, and Modern English. Middle English was spoken between about 1066 and the mid-1400s. It is different from Modern English, but with effort we can sometimes figure it out. Believe it or not, the great English writer William Shakespeare wrote in Modern English. It was very early Modern English. We can see examples of English from the past by reading old books. Look at the quotes on these pages. Can you figure them out?

> Whan that the knight hadde thus his tale ytold,
> In al the route nas ther yong ne old
> That he ne saide it was a noble storye,
> And worthy for to drawen to memorye,
> And namely the gentils everichoon.

Geoffrey Chaucer (about 1343–1400), Middle English

> My father watches,—O sir! Fly this place;
> Intelligence is given where you are hid:
> You have now the good advantage of the night,—
> Have you not spoken 'gainst the Duke of Cornwall?
> He's coming hither; now, i' the night, i' the haste,
> And Regan with him:

William Shakespeare (1564–1616), Early Modern English

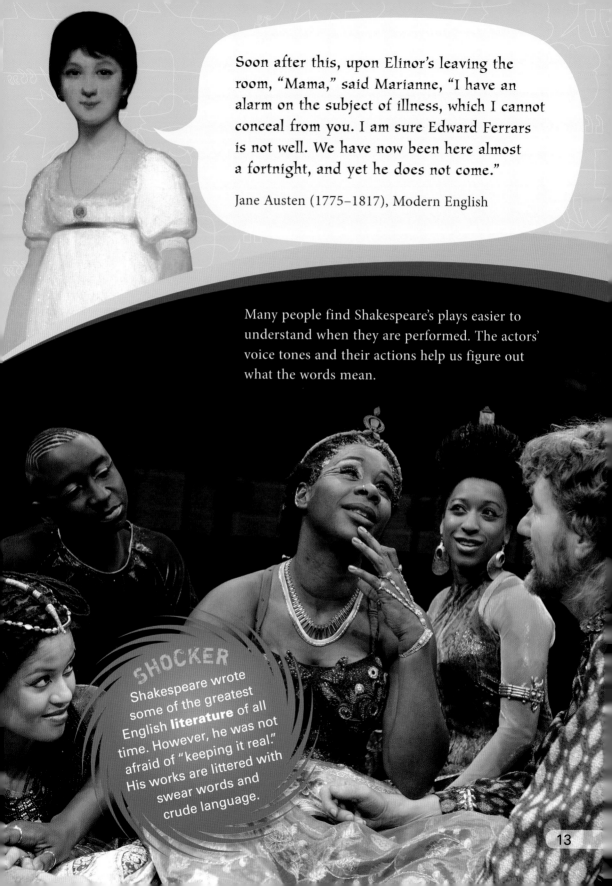

Soon after this, upon Elinor's leaving the room, "Mama," said Marianne, "I have an alarm on the subject of illness, which I cannot conceal from you. I am sure Edward Ferrars is not well. We have now been here almost a fortnight, and yet he does not come."

Jane Austen (1775–1817), Modern English

Many people find Shakespeare's plays easier to understand when they are performed. The actors' voice tones and their actions help us figure out what the words mean.

SHOCKER
Shakespeare wrote some of the greatest English **literature** of all time. However, he was not afraid of "keeping it real!" His works are littered with swear words and crude language.

13

The Generation Gap

English is still changing at a fast pace. New words are constantly entering the language. Some words are made up from parts of old words. *Camcorder*, for example, is made up from *camera* and *recorder*. We're still picking up plenty of new words from other languages too. Words such as *khaki*, *poncho*, and *sushi* are all new to English.

Got some new glad rags? They're the cat's pajamas!

1920s

We've gotta win today, or we kiss the trophy good-bye!

1930s

People have always used **slang** to show that they're cool or "hip."

We had a blast at Joe's party. It was coolsville!

1950s

Dig this music! It's far out!

1960s

Sometimes old words take on new meanings. For example, *cool* has meant "slightly cold" for hundreds of years. But in the 1930s, jazz musicians started using it to mean "good" or "fashionable." By the 1950s, young people were using it this way too. Many parents were horrified. They thought it was "bad" English. Even today, some people see changes as a sign of damage to the language. However, with a vibrant language such as English, change is continual and unavoidable.

New words come from ...
- parts of old words
- other languages
- new uses for old words
- advances in science and technology

Jazz is cool!

Did You Know?

Most slang words go out of fashion and disappear. Others become part of the language. Some old slang words that are now accepted are *piano*, *scary*, *snooze*, *fun*, *clever*, and *okay*.

People have always feared change. Ranulph Higden, who lived in England in the 1300s, had this to say:

... by intermingling and mixing, first with Danes and afterwards with Normans, in many people the language of the land is harmed, and some use strange inarticulate utterance, chattering, snarling, and harsh teeth-gnashing.

Shifting Meanings

Many words have more than one meaning. Just take a look at a dictionary. Sometimes a word will start out with one meaning and then pick up new meanings as people start being creative with it. For example, a *princess* used to mean exclusively the daughter of a king or queen. Today, an ordinary young woman might be described as a princess if she is fussed over a great deal.

Princess Haya is a real princess. Her late father was the king of Jordan.

The word *princess* often conjures up an image of a glamorous woman in fairy-tale clothing.

Some people get called a princess just because they act like a princess – a spoiled one, that is.

Some words start to lose their full meanings. These days *fantastic*, *awesome*, *terrific*, *cool*, and *incredible* all mean "really good." In the past, they each had very different meanings. *Fantastic* meant "something made up; a fantasy." *Awesome* meant "inspiring **awe**." *Terrific* first meant "terrifying," then it meant "very large." Now it usually just means "good."

I have to look something up on the Web, but my mouse is broken!

Meanings also depend on how things are said. "Oh, terrific!" usually means "That's really good." But it can mean "really bad." Usually a person's tone of voice gives it away.

Many of the words we use for computers were known hundreds of years ago. They just weren't used in the way we use them now. *Mouse*, *Web*, *printer*, and *monitor* are just some examples. Can you think of any others?

SHOCKER

Some words have changed over time to mean the opposite of what they used to mean. *Brave* used to mean "cowardly." *Manufacture* once meant "to make something by hand."

Why Spelling Is Hard

Why spelling is Hard

Do you find spelling difficult? If so, it's not surprising. Learning to spell in English is harder than in many other languages. This is partly because many words aren't spelled the way they are **pronounced**. Look at *knee*, *eight*, and *ache*, for example. But did you know that these words are spelled the way they used to be pronounced?

After the printing press was invented in the 1400s, spelling became fixed, but the way people pronounced words continued to change. In the past, the final *e* on words such as *name* and *house* was pronounced "uh," as it often is in *the*. The *e* in the *-ed* word ending was also pronounced. *Moved*, for example, was pronounced "moo-vid."

Back in the **Middle Ages**, we always pronounced the *k* in *knee*, *knife*, and *knight*. We called a knee a "kuh nee," which made spelling easier!

The heading on this page told me what to expect on the rest of the page. Headings like these make reading easier. They just don't make spelling any easier!

How do we know how people used to pronounce things? Linguists figure it out by studying old writing. Bad spellers usually write words the way they say them. This provides clues. Rhyme also gives us hints about pronunciation. Shakespeare's poems imply that in his day *devil* and *evil* rhymed, as did *knees* and *grease*.

ENGLISH LANGUAGE PROFESSOR

Fantastic! This old document was written by a terrible speller!

LEICESTER SQUARE

In England, some old place names have changed their pronunciation so much over time that they sound nothing like their spelling. Take a look at these place names.

Leicester	*LESS tuh*
Warwick	*WOH rik*
Seven Oaks	*SNOAKS*
Worcester	*WOH stuh*
Hertford	*HART fid*
Gloucester	*GLOSS ta*

19

Accents and Dialects

As soon as you start speaking, you give clues about where you come from. The particular way you pronounce your words is called your accent. Most of the people living in the same area have the same accent. Can you tell a British accent from an American accent? How is a New York accent different from a Tennessee accent?

As well as speaking in different accents, English speakers from a particular area often use some of their own words and ways of putting words together. These words and phrases, along with the accent, make up a region's **dialect**. Scottish people, for example, have their own dialect of English. At its most extreme, it can seem like another language. Take a look at the poem by Scottish poet Robert Burns, on the opposite page.

> In the first paragraph, the author seemed to be asking me questions. I don't think she really wanted me to answer them. This is just an interesting way of pointing out some different accents.

You say "tuh MAH toe."

And you say "tuh MAY toe."

Last year, we moved from London to Chicago. Some kids made fun of my accent. I picked up a Chicago accent as fast as I could.

I liked having a different accent. I got a lot of extra attention. Sadly, I'm losing my old accent now.

As an adult, it is hard for me to change the way I speak. I'll probably always sound British, whether I want to or not.

Young people often pick up new accents faster than older people.

Think You Know English?

Take a look at these Scottish words.

Scottish English	Standard English
aboot	about
loch	lake
lassie	girl
tattie	potato
bairn	child
galoot	fool

To a Mouse

Wee sleekit, cow'rin, tim'rous beastie,
O, what a panic's in thy breastie!
Thou need na start awa sae hasty,
Wi bickering brattle!
I wad be laith to rin an chase thee,
Wi murdering pattle!

Robert Burns (1759–1796)

21

In the past, the many towns and villages in the British Isles had their own accents and dialects. From the 1500s onward, people from Britain and Ireland began **emigrating** around the world. Different groups tended to settle in different places. Many Irish people, for example, settled in Chicago. The different mix of people in each place influenced the accent and dialect that developed there.

Today's American English has words that used to be spoken in England, but no longer are. For example, in Shakespeare's day, *autumn* was often called *fall*. In the United States, that season is usually called *fall*. In England, however, *fall* is rarely used. The American pronunciation of the word *bath* used to be spoken all over England. Today, it is pronounced "barth" in southern England.

SHOCKER

The English invaded Ireland in the 1100s and later took control of the country. English became the language of the country's rulers. Everyone was encouraged to speak English, and the Irish language nearly died out altogether. It was English, not Irish, that Irish **immigrants** took to the New World.

What do you call this? That depends on where you live. In New York, you might call it a hero. In Louisiana, you might call it a po' boy. In other places, it may be called a submarine, a hoagie, a filled roll, a torpedo, a grinder, a zeppelin, or simply a sandwich.

22

British and American tourists can get very confused when shopping in each other's countries. Often the same word means something different in each place.

Jumper
Pinafore
Sweater
Jumper

U.S. English	British English
gasoline	petrol
cookie	biscuit
faucet	tap
elevator	lift
diaper	nappy
flashlight	torch
apartment	flat
candy	sweets
cell phone	mobile phone
pacifier	dummy

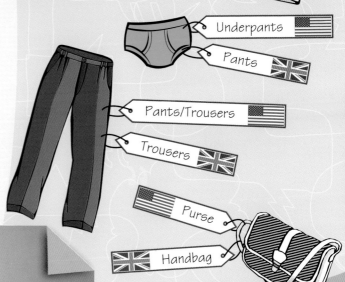

Underpants
Pants
Pants/Trousers
Trousers
Purse
Handbag

English is complex because …
- meanings keep changing
- different words are used in different places
- new words keep getting added
- spelling is very tricky
- there are different accents and dialects

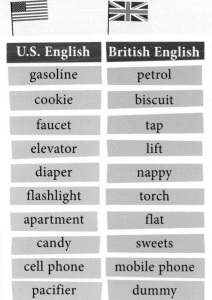

The phrase *bring a dish* actually means "bring a dish with some tasty food on it." Many a new immigrant has turned up at a potluck supper with an empty plate and been very embarrassed.

Formal and Informal English

The way we speak is often more relaxed than the way we write. When speaking to friends, we often leave words out, blur them together, and include lots of slang. Newspapers and books are usually written more **formally**.

In reality, there is no single correct way to speak or write English. However, there is a dialect of English that many people think represents the language. This is sometimes called Standard English. It is most broadly broken down into British Standard English and American Standard English. Some people try to describe these varieties of English. They publish books filled with rules to help writers use them. The books list rules about **grammar**, spelling, and **punctuation**. Teachers often like us to stick to these rules too.

Imagine if newscasters spoke in informal English. They might sound a bit like this newscaster. However, newscasters usually try to speak in standard English. It makes them sound more official and believable.

Yeah, so, um, the President, he was like, "I'm not gonna stand for this." And then, the other politician, um, what's her name? Anyway, she was like …

In British Standard English, the word *color* is spelled *colour*. However, there is no letter *u* in the American spelling of *color*. Publishers often produce different versions of the same book for Britain and the United States.

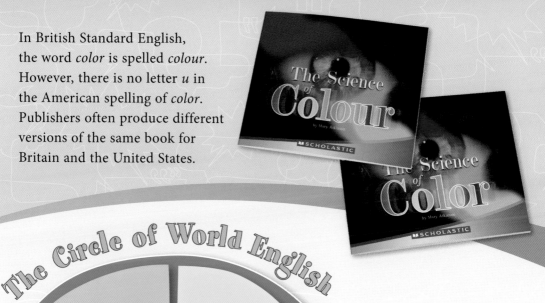

The Circle of World English

American English

British and Irish English

Canadian English

Australian, New Zealand and Pacific Island English

World Standard English

West, East, and Southern African English

East Asian English

Caribbean English

South Asian English

This circle shows the **diversity** of the English language. Each segment can be broken down even further. For example, Canadian English includes Inuit English, Ukrainian English, and Newfoundland English.

Many Inuit people in Canada speak both their native language, Inuktitut, and English. When speaking in English, they sometimes use Inuktitut words.

Quirky Expressions

English has plenty of tricky features that can make learning difficult. For example, it has many idioms. These are **expressions** that have a specific meaning that can't be inferred simply from the words themselves. For example, we could say, "The thief was caught red-handed." This idiom means that the thief was caught in the act of stealing something. It doesn't mean that the thief **literally** had red hands. To understand an idiom, you have to learn it. When you are new to the language, this can be hard work.

Like many other languages, English also has plenty of proverbs. These are often sayings that have been handed down through the generations. Proverbs often describe observations about human nature. *Nothing ventured, nothing gained,* for example, tells us that we won't get anywhere if we don't try. *Children should be seen and not heard,* on the other hand, has gone out of fashion.

The rat race is an idiom. It doesn't usually have anything to do with rats or races. Instead, it is a name for the long, busy days of hardworking business people.

Nose-y Idioms

Who "nose" what they mean?

Follow your nose!

It's right under your nose.

Don't look down your nose at me!

It's no skin off my nose.

Don't rub his nose in it.

She has her nose in the air.

Other "body part" idioms include: *feet of clay, bee's knees, eye candy, ear for music,* and *stiff upper lip.*

Have you heard the proverb, *The grass is always greener on the other side of the hill*? It describes the tendency of people to think that whatever they do not have must be better than what they do have.

What's in a Name?

We use names to identify people and pets. We also name countries, cities, streets, rivers, and mountains. Most names have a meaning. However, many meanings are lost over time. Some first names, such as Elizabeth and Jacob, were originally Hebrew names found in the Bible. Can you guess where names such as Rose, Daisy, and Jasmine come from? Many names, such as Luisa and Ravi, have been adopted from other languages. Some names are simply made up by people who like the sound of them.

In the early Middle Ages, most English people didn't have **surnames**. The first surnames described people. Someone called Johnson would have been the son of John. Peter York would have come from the town of York. Names such as Short, Young, and Moody described people's personality or looks. Other names, such as Miller and Shepherd, described people's jobs.

SHOCKER

Mount Misery, Mount Difficult, Poverty Bay, and Doubtful River are names of real places in New Zealand! Happily, there are also the Bay of Plenty, Hope River, and Mount Solution.

Homesick immigrants often name new towns after the place they come from. Portsmouth, New Hampshire, for example, is named after the English city of Portsmouth and the nearby county of Hampshire.

Names come and go in fashion. Here are some popular names from the last century.

1900s	1940s	1960s	1980s	2000s
Elsie	Margaret	Jennifer	Jessica	Brittany
Edith	Janet	Karen	Ashley	Madison
Mildred	Patricia	Amanda	Katherine	Jasmine
Arthur	Michael	Steven	Joshua	Tyler
Frank	Richard	Jeffrey	Daniel	Ryan
Samuel	Brian	Robert	Matthew	Ethan

Some first names have meanings that are not obvious. For example, the name *Melissa* means "honeybee," and the name *Greg* means "watchful."

Some of the descendants of **medieval** cooks and bakers have the surname Cook or Baker today.

Letters, E-mails, and Texts

Before telephones, people often spent time writing letters to each other. Good writers wrote detailed letters about their thoughts and feelings, and about the events in their lives. Often, the letters of famous people were published in books after they had died. Even today, people enjoy these glimpses into past lives.

In the 1980s, many teachers worried that the art of letter writing was dying out. Most young people hardly ever wrote letters. They used the telephone instead. However, the rise of the Internet changed all that. Now we e-mail our friends or write to organizations all the time. If we own a cell phone, we send text messages too. Many people find it easier to send an electronic note than to talk on the phone or face-to-face. Now some teachers are worried that even the art of conversation may die out.

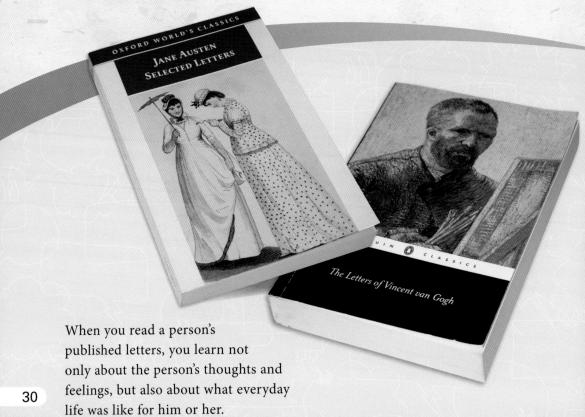

When you read a person's published letters, you learn not only about the person's thoughts and feelings, but also about what everyday life was like for him or her.

Before voice-recording devices, secretaries had to take notes from dictation. Because it was hard to keep up if they wrote in **longhand**, shorthand was invented. In shorthand languages, some symbols stand for sounds, not letters. For example, ⌐ can stand for the sound "th."

Text messages are expensive and hard to type on tiny keypads. To save money and effort, people often write text messages in "text languages." Can you work out what this message means?

8:39am

a

Gr8 2 c u. R u
goin 2 ftball l8r?
cya s%n

Continue   More

Electronic Communication

Pros	Cons
• quicker	• conversation
• easier	dying out
• instant	• can be expensive
response	• less face-to-face
	contact

Many young people send each other e-mails and text messages in text language. Sometimes they even use text language in their schoolwork. Most teachers, however, do not accept work in text language. They think that it is important that students learn how to write and spell in Standard English. This will help them communicate confidently when they grow up.

WHAT DO YOU THINK?

Should students be allowed to hand in schoolwork written in text language rather than Standard English?

PRO

I think we should be allowed to write in text language. We all understand it, and it is quick. This is just a natural change, like the other changes through history. People should accept it, not fight it. It doesn't hurt anyone.

There are many versions of text language. Friends often know and understand the shortened words and symbols that they use with each other. However, figuring out unfamiliar words can be hard work, and it takes time. Some people think that this spoils the pleasure of reading. If books were in text language, they might take longer to read than in Standard English.

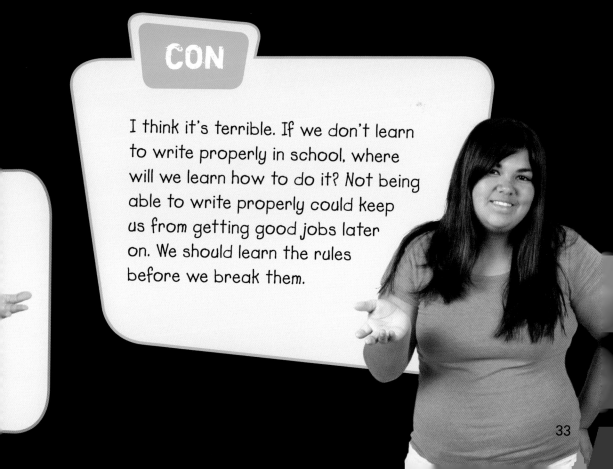

CON

I think it's terrible. If we don't learn to write properly in school, where will we learn how to do it? Not being able to write properly could keep us from getting good jobs later on. We should learn the rules before we break them.

GLOSSARY

awe a mixture of admiration and fear

dialect (*DYE uh lekt*) a way that a language is spoken in a particular place

diversity (*di VUR suh tee*) variety

emigrate (*EM uh grate*) to leave one country to live in another

expression a phrase that has a particular meaning

formally in a proper way; not casually

immigrant (*IM uh gruhnt*) a person who has moved to a new country

Latin the language of the ancient Romans

literature written works such as novels, plays, and poems

longhand the usual way of writing sentences, in which every word is written in full

medieval to do with the Middle Ages

Middle Ages the period in European history from about 500 A.D. to about 1500 A.D.

monk a man who lives in a religious community

Normans people from Normandy, which is now a region in northern France

surname a last name or family name

Viking one of the Scandinavian warriors who invaded European countries between 800 A.D. and 1100 A.D.

Monk

FIND OUT MORE

BOOKS

Baker, Rosalie F. *In a Word: 750 Words and Their Fascinating Stories and Origins*. Cobblestone Publishing, 2003.

Brocker, Susan. *Paper Trail: History of an Everyday Material*. Scholastic Inc., 2008.

O'Conner, Patricia T. *Woe Is I Jr.: The Younger Grammarphobe's Guide to Better English in Plain English*. Putnam, 2007.

O'Reilly, Gillian. *Slangalicious: Where We Got That Crazy Lingo*. Annick Press, 2004.

Robb, Don. *Ox, House, Stick: The History of Our Alphabet*. Charlesbridge Publishing, 2007.

WEB SITES

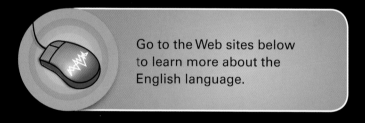

Go to the Web sites below to learn more about the English language.

www.bbc.co.uk/history/british/lang_gallery.shtml

www.niehs.nih.gov/kids/jokeengl.htm#languag

www.factmonster.com/ipka/A0769301.html

www.funbrain.com/words.html

INDEX

ABOUT THE AUTHOR

Mary Atkinson is the author of many fiction and nonfiction books for children. She has worked as a writer and editor for eighteen years. However, her love of books and writing goes back even further than that. As a child, she discovered the pleasure of losing herself in a great story and soon developed a fascination with words and their origins. Having lived in New Zealand, England, and the United States, Mary has experienced firsthand the many problems that can arise when people with different accents and dialects attempt to communicate.